"This" Ameri-can-*ah*

"This" Ameri-can-*ah*

poems by

CURTIS L. GRISLER

Cherry Castle Publishing

Cover Image: "Fiftyless" © 2015 by Melissa Vandenberg
Section Images: (american us) "Proper Patriot,"
(becoming beautiful) "Slanted Patriot," (deep life)
"Disorderly Conduct" © 2015 by Melissa Vandenberg

Cover Design: Deb Dulin
Edited by Truth Thomas & Melanie Henderson
Copy Editor: Susan Thornton Hobby
Author Photograph: © 2015 by William "Bryant" Rozier

All rights reserved.
Published in the United States of America
First published as a Cherry Castle paperback 2015

ISBN-10: 0-692-57208-2
ISBN-13: 978-0-692-57208-5
#
Library of Congress Control Number: 2015956676

Cherry Castle Publishing, LLC
P. O. Box 6355
Columbia, MD 21045
www.cherrycastlepublishing.com
where words grow mighty trees

ACKNOWLEDGEMENTS

The author would like to thank the Cherry Castle Publishing family, the City of Asylum/Pittsburgh (COA/P), Cave Canem, the Indiana Arts Commission, IPFW for providing needed funding, sanctuary, and/or guidance, as well as the editors of the following publications, in which these poems first appeared:

AAR (African American Review) "Red Lights (Before the Closing of Kroger)"
anti-, Issue #5 "They will say"
Crab Orchard Review, Vol. 15 No. 2 "american us"
Dare To Dream…Change The World (anthology) "Jean-Michel Basquiat's Boyhood Song"
Facing Homelessness in Fort Wayne: A Story Telling Project to Increase Awareness. "For the man in the last pew"
Golden Shovel (anthology) "Tuesday's divorce cramps"
HEArt "becoming beautiful"
In The Eye: a collection of writings "Sound" and "Black Whiskers"
Kweli Journal (Fall/ Winter 2009) "Oscar"
Ocean Voices (anthology) "deep life"
pluck! "poet juice"
Sou'wester "If Miles played for Barack (on Swearing in Day)"
The November 3rd Club "Overflow"
The Margin, Vol. 1, Issue 3 "Identity Thief," originally titled "Lupus"
Tidal Basin Review "9/11/2010" and "Catching Train"
Tipton Poetry Review "Blessed rancor of music"

CONTENTS

ACKNOWLEDGEMENTS — v
FOREWORD — xiii

"american us"

If Miles played for Barack (on Swearing-in Day) — 3
Silhouette — 5
Catching Train — 7
For the man in the last pew — 8
Shopping from the dead — 10
On a drive-by, he gave me life — 12
mamie till's whispers caught on magnolia grandiflora — 13
Red Lights (Before the Closing of Kroger) — 14
Waiting for small connections between cities — 15
Overflow — 17
american us — 19
Tuesday's divorce cramps — 20
They ~~will~~ say — 21
poet juice — 23
Saturday — 24
Working class insteps — 25
Crossing Over the Road Not Taken — 27
in that box on (5933 bunt) — 28
Duen-day — 29

"becoming beautiful"

Throwdown (reflections on fighting) — 33
"I brought you into this world …" — 34
Living just enough for the city — 35

January 31, 2012 (night eye)	36
becoming beautiful	37
indiana saffron	39
Amish Swag	40
them teacher smoke breaks	41
Blessed rancor of music	42
Jean-Michel Basquiat's Boyhood Song	44
The closest I got to superhero	45

"deep life"

9/11/2010	51
deep life	53
Oscar	55
Sound	56
Velvet shock therapy	58
Identity Thief	59
Black Whiskers	61
block party	62
A train is gon' come (elegy for the big afro)	64
The third child	66
Awake	68
Gangsta love	69
Midwest hang, man	70
A Pen Pal with HIV Gets Lost in Shuffle	72
Six dandelions beg for some sun, off the I-65	73
Magic Man	77

ABOUT THE AUTHOR 80

*For my maverick family, and all its permutations.
You are always with me.*

"This" Ameri-can-*ah*

In memory of Deborah K. Littlejohn
September 17, 1948 - December 27, 2011

FOREWORD

i.
America is a nun in her habit purchasing Mickey D's in O'Hare Airport. America is capitalism for service. "Serve us"— serve us. Did cheese smother what she had on her mind? Here, trade and religion merge like car lanes. Dark and light faces fast foot the middle of concourses, sounding like Sandman Sims' soft-shoeing his anger, reaching another concourse with time. Here, time isn't worried about flight. Time's not the gateway drug from here to there. This is here, America. America, here.

ii.
We arrive and depart like the red C pointing out directions — the ghost of Christmas future. We all should be in H, not in stasis, not on tarmac where big birds are scared that little birds will bring them down — how fleet light feathers stop steel engine turbines. We are the *e pluribus*, the mean moaning *unum*.

iii.
The barefoot Asian girl plops her feet on the tile floor, got black soles. A white man got crew cut, got handlebar moustache, kicking time in New Balance. The eye goes to the crème-colored bald boy with little tufts of hair on his dome — a grandma's withered garden — the pain of dust bowls. Eyes stick to him. I's erect. The bald boy, with little tufts of hair, hands out Hare Krishna smiles, leaves cancer back in the terminal.

"american us"

"The museum of escaped lightning"
—Eric Baus

If Miles played for Barack (on Swearing-in Day)

He'd start his morning with push
ups — tonguing a gold mouthpiece

    fifty times in succession — all evil
in him washing up against the round surf

of his big canine eyes, where one tear
hesitates. Miles would play to conceptualize

    this *new* day. He'd temper scales —
prayers for forgiveness to women

he held captive to the madness of
his confliction — beauty. His will now,

    translating sacred Paris notes to
his lone prayer, "God please save a fool."

Hate was locked up in a historic key.
A door stayed shut. While he was so blue

    he'd sit outside of it, transcribing
the small intel God gave him, itty-bitty

illuminations — how to breathe —
what to smell — who owned the sun.

    His anger would escalator down,
erode into acid reflux, rumble above or through

his groin, reminding him that the bass's
pulse was a hot throb back in hard cotton fields,

 back two migrations north, back to
grandmother's motherland. He plays with what

to sport in front of the Lincoln Memorial,
how his suit will pop, clash, blend into harsh marble:

 horn screaming at birds, trains, all walking life.

Silhouette
— *For Eugene Allen, the butler, R.I.P.*

You, whose shadow still stains the other side of the Oval Office door;
you who sat in dustless silence, waiting for Air Force

    One's tires to touch earth. You who served quail in white
truffle sauce and clean Scotch with milk for a president's sour

stomach. You who stayed up past midnight to give hot
chocolate to a president's child who saw you as "other,"

    when all you were doing was the work, wanting
to make your Helene blush when embraced. How you own

each little step to striving. You knew the glib falsehood of
the Left and the Right, so circumvented back to King standing

    in the corridor of that hallowed white building. The reverend
talked you into compliments, like soothing handmade rosaries

the Pope pockets. You grab the beads in your mind,
like petals from Godiva roses kissing your tongue. You own

    the voices of men and women who burn or balm all ears,
but you only listen to the voice of comfort — the one

in the frontier of your heart. For you, there is only the issue of
tracing the hand over aching heart murmurs, like a tired head circles

    the pillow, looking for a clearing. The best housewarming gift was Helene,
sixty-five years of her touch — her jasmine propulsion

cloaking you from one threshold to the next. In your head,
she resides in the promise she made after her voice stopped

ricocheting walls of your house. Before enrolling into morning, you mouth *Helene*, kiss the wall she painted aqua, head out for 1600

Pennsylvania, to shake hands with our first brown-faced president. He will welcome you back. You will cry for Helene.

Catching Train

We three stepped back on train platform
as the wildness in the red-haired drunk

man wanted our audience. His woman,
appalled, opposite platform, facing us,

showed how fear played with death on her
face, when love sat there a minute before —

tenor sax riff. Sparks were expected. Talk
of a third rail jumps out a child's mouth, small

boy who never knew stupidity had red-hair,
freckles — flat piano chords. Danger arched

our minds like 3D streamers in a hot Chinese
New Year celebration. But no flashes. Mr.

Freckles stumbled before all, waiting for D.C.'s
Red Line to screech over his woman's loud

embarrassment. That fast, danger evaporated.
What's hot transformed to something cold.

The train swallowed us. Lodged in its teeth,
we held onto leather tonsils. Were we Jonahs,

or were we Pinocchios looking for ways to
make inanimate a human touch? Death

shrank from big to small — the air burnt
stale with a light halitosis of mixed breathing,

with streaks strident down hot rails — the night's
blue — a woman tasting tears on platform.

For the man in the last pew
— *the man with the same name as mine*

"It's a little thing for me to live through these cards.
They show the places that make my mind smile —

    places I'd live in if I knew magic, or didn't have
    the job of owning all of the dreams of my past.

Christmas cards are easier to live in. I've collected more
than 3,000 cards since 1985. The reds and the blues

    that glitter have a different meaning when I
    can put my hands on the edges of their frames.

People make me scratch my head. People poke me
and it scrunches my mind. And people forget people

    are not all hard. When in state's hands, I thought
    I would miss people, but the medicine made me

only depend on the movies in my mind, scenes where
Mama sat in our living room, while I read how the words

    in the Bible move in this life, without the worry
    of her suffering. Suffering comes like daylight

into my bedroom, now, taking me out of the darkness,
into creaky pews of Mission Church on Pearl Street.

    I bring with me Mama memories — the birthday
    and Christmas cards I hand out to the worn faces

I have come to smile at in my comeback to the world.
I could be a mad dog about it all, but I have food, the

warmth of my apartment, and how God put new
light in my head. The new moved out the old,

and no institution can own my me, now. I accept all
my nightmares, and I don't mind shaking off any dust."

Shopping from the dead

    My sister ushered over her father's clothes,
the only man I would ever call "Daddy"   After

    she left   I turned my livingroom and bedroom
and bathroom into a changingroom   fumbling

    through his colorwheel of fashion   *This is how I
extend my wardrobe*   as I tried on the cashmere over-

    coat I will have Toskos   my Greek tailor   take in at
the waist   along with the black double-breasted sports

    coat   even if I avoid double-breasted custody   *It fits
except his arms were an inch or two longer*   What I found

    in his pockets   a banana split Dum Dums wrapper
a receipt from Community Financial from 2008

    a wrapper for a Reese's chocolate-covered peanut
butter egg   two Reese's mini-chocolate eggs

    two Easter gummy eggs   one Arcor Tutti Bol hard
candy   and a small tan envelope full of air   How

    I connected to the missing missive he folded like a
handkerchief   or ten dollar bills   How I wonder

    what Easter did his candy come from   It still looked
good enough to consume   I see logic like Sherlock —

    see this as his last Easter   I put all the candy in
the plastic bag   *Wonder if I should send this*

debris back to my sister   "Debris" a noun I play with
to shop from the dead   A necromancer pickpocket to

   the someone I once touched   How am I sleeping
under the quilt of a family's story   a wedding dress

   slacks of my soldier grandfather   a toddler's
baptismal garment   This mortgage   I now own

   What's on my back   the full weight of a man's
existence   how to wear his days like a monk's robe

On a drive-by, he gave me life

On my cool down, he rolls up on
me, cig in hand, two limbs missing.
Croaks out, "I had to sneak out
to get a smoke." His face scrunches
so tough, the preview of his life
wears him like a jailhouse tattoo.
My mind sees doorknobs, pirates,
soldiers returning from Afghanistan.
"You have to do what you have to
do." I return some change, bounce
on the two legs my Gary mother and
Chicago father supplied. I look at
ash trees that survived the war with
ash worms. I try to decipher birds'
nests from squirrels' nests on a cutting
October morning, where leaves say
so much more than they ever said,
up to this point. I refuse to look back.
His electric chair rolls on, cig smoke
grabbing at the crispness of
synergy — stuck in the same Tuesday
of all Tuesdays, bound to not recoil.

mamie till's whispers caught on magnolia grandiflora

        the longest one ever feels —
     tallahatchie deep.   *can we bend*
                     into each other's border
wet notes stretching to silty shore.
           find how two
     the always drowning —   *become us*
    the always death
        of anything —   *lose it all*
      the song's breathing.   *on a wind?*

"american us"

Red Lights (Before the Closing of Kroger)
— *For Paul, John, Ringo, George, Roxy*

There are places I'll remember all
my life though some have changed ... blares
from the driver's side, a sunburnt bearded
man's mint-conditioned purple Impala. *Damn,*
that ride's sweet. How our utterances will drive
smack into air like the sparrow veering into a new
direction. On the passenger side of day, T-Pain
and Lil Wayne pull alongside in booming clarion
of swagger — the hot thump of bump and ghetto
fabulousness — clanking Ballers giving rhythm
to a small city. Catty-corner Kroger occupies
blue collars who walk to get sustenance, no food —
a free connection for sweet reciprocity, to not
assuage oneself to a dank room, solitary confinement.
We visualize neighbors who chat beyond the silence
of a good job, of how a lawn's so greenest green,
a Streisand song couldn't handle it — since the big
water shortage of the late '80s. Our houses draw
character like our music. We are different types
of rats in the same amazement for peanut butter, for
cheese. The wind mends us, makes us take off
our open-toed sandals, drive all "country," foot
out the window, slapped by hot obstinate wind,
feeling gas pedal oscillate speed, feeling vibration,
the warm leg of our woman touch ours — to not let
go, to keep motion neutral for *people and things that*
went before: dad's souped-up Chevy on our 22-
inch chrome rims — nothing else moves. Norman
Rockwell haggles with Russell Simmons on Abbey
Road; a violet Midwest, full-grown, knows its
mirror, knows tomorrow won't slide left or die.

"This" Ameri-can-*ah*

Waiting for small connections between cities

Smelling Air Canada Regional Jet fumes
let's your stomach know if it can stand to

fly or not fly. The stomach will accept
only so much discombobulating

before sending back uneaten brunch with
its utensils and dishware on the dumbwaiter.

The sour taste of throwing up in your mouth,
just a touch, is like waves coming to shore,

just so much. The exhaust fumes bouquet
like spring's cherry blossoms jumping in your

eyes — the white hats of new Sunday in D.C.
Now, you know you will never be Chuck Yeager.

Now, you know you will never be a Red Tail.
Hell, you won't even make it as a Maverick

with a kickass Hollywood soundtrack pushing
you "past danger." As you cover your nose

you grasp the authentic you, the English major,
the one teaching words to those who fly,

to those who can taste the firm in firmament —
the blue, the white, like all hawks, all seagulls.

You maneuver across concourse, gaining a
small taste of the turkey burger you ate

earlier. You are not downed. You are not flaming out. *You* bend words into lives that

live. Most get grounded. Some take sky.

Overflow

The golden bell of the trumpet
punched C's above scale into cold
and windy graveyard air. Dresses
of women blew rayon ripples to
an east. Bare legs surfaced chill
bumps, longing for the warmth of
a bed where room's heat whistles
and rumbles — a grumbling ghost.
"Taps" sliced through his Native
American ears, a knife so sharp
when cutting, the pain of the blood
does not recognize its own hand in
the deed. A strong lonely lodges
in his belly, and he cannot see sky.
Life left him within his own mind,
never knowing his white father who
garnered ceremonial garb, put into
a plot under the great arm of idyllic
birch. His mother wore a lazy smile,
sat next to a deluxe casket. Soldiers
handed her triangle flag — a flag that
belongs to so many dead and living
hands. Rumble. It all rumbled.
Tears gathered — he blamed wind.
No. It was "Taps." It always stuck
raw in his throat for all those feral
young boys who never got a chance
to seed more feral boys. He knew
the trumpet was a malicious home-
wrecker, who called The Duke —
a Calvary on his ancestors — a hot
lover, Louis Armstrong loved all of
his existence, fighting to grow music
out of tragedy. But how does a son

solve the puzzle of being Army, Apache,
German — living on rez? It burns to
not wipe eyes, a wet fighting down
his cheeks. The crowd believed he's
moved by stiff mother's face, by the
sharpness of wind striking red skin,
shaking off killer throbs, but blinded
between ancestors and government,
his haze washed-out to widest cobalt
he could never tame.

american us

— *For those crazy noodlers*

He beats chest, a usually shy adolescent,
sporting new Sean John b-ball cap, raising
a catfish, his body length, to be on camera.
No one could call him pusillanimous, since
his father taught him the hundred-year-old
art, where a subculture of bare-handed badasses
search the dark-ridden cubby-holes of muddy
waters, avoiding teeth, feeling for gums and
whiskers of flat-heads in a soupy darkened bank
of Oklahoma's sub-earth, where the two-toned
black and silver fish hide and wait to bite arms

of the men foolish enough to "Catfist." This is a place
where all sons dream in watercolor. Men here
are men — good ole boys with protruding cheeks

full of snuff, wearing five-gallon hats or Nascar
caps, jaw-yapping about copperhead bites, or
letting a flat-head loose to mar the forearm into
a permanent tattoo of scar tissue. The brave ones
have signed up at Bob's Pig Shop for the huge
contest, where the young boy sees his father as
a warrior with water — loving every soaked fiber
of his Dad's favorite Wranglers, or Levi's, letting
the murky water lease him for an integer in time,
until long black whiskers slap and wrap up his
elbow like wet shoestrings. A father owns a smile,
and his son extols his infection, and smiles new.

Tuesday's divorce cramps
— *A Golden Shovel after Antoinette Brim*

On the other side of *that* window
to my soul, she always blinds the
frowns in my heavy eyes — a slice
of wonder left like lone maple leaf on the
doorstep in spring, where the sun
runs away from the rain, here, into
snatches of gray. There are no lemon-
yellow-things in bloom, or the smell of pie
slapping the nose to attention. It's the wedges
inside me she's compartmentalized, and
how those wedges weep. I must then
carry on with what happens to the splatters
a wedge can leave behind — the sticky of them
stepped upon — a body moved onto
the next aching moment, holding up all else in the
world. I tilt back on my only support — a wall.

They will say
— R.I.P. JMJ

you are flash in pan, and have been talkin'
ish since The Sugarhill Gang — ole school fool.

They will say, "You're loud, angry when bumpin',
and we can't understand your words." *[The rule*

to code switchin' is to switch codes: you must
trust odd prophets spreadin' good news]. It's true

Shanté, Latifah, Salt-N-Pepa fussed
that their "disease" couldn't be saved with a pill.

Malcolm mused out, "Don't know if I could start
a riot, but I don't know if I would

stop one." They will say rap lingo burns hard:
pimp, bitch, ho — our art and women abused

and splayed like hot meat on a barbecue-
mesquite-Sunday, when just hangin' with crew.

~~~

Your crew can understand, to a point, with
mess that's on BET and MTV,

folk might hear small requiem-side of myth —
a dead-end-corner slangin' broke-back-beats,

not the pissed-off-to-all-pisstivity
of Chuck D's third eye. They want glamor's rise,

and Beasties not illin' now. Streets got peeps
who graduated Hollis, *rock it like*

"american us"

this, who got Harvard degrees in puttin'-
it-on-ya. The HOT playlist so wicked,

spinnin' butt-lick-flick-jams that's cold dissin'
KRS-One, and Bambaataa's magic —

just gettin' hip to ole school, think Common
on "new kick," but he dressed-up son-of-Run.

~~~

All sons-of-Run jam it within hot rim-
shots like Kweli, beg for sunbeams to line

our foreheads. Ziggy Marley, "Jah love him,"
singing jaunty from death-boxes of pine —

feeds us hearty refrains. Now, Jill Scott trusts;
Lauryn Hill trusts too — got *crazy love* for

set-free minds, while hyped Mos Def marches us
beyond bouncing black booties — airtime whores

for glitz, bucks, status — back into what is
hip hip-hop, where The Roots sleep and funk up

purity through drums, bass, and horns; all this
so Angie Stone can cold blend world's corrup-

tions through melody. Naysayers say, "this
ish, that ish." We so hot, go straight R-E-M-I-X!

"This" Ameri-can-*ah*

poet juice

"Do not come lightly to the page"
— *Nikky Finney*

*not until you sleep on a futon in a n.y. apt
w/ an ex-con who's had poetry beat him down in

a cell of etheridge knightmares does forgiveness
metastasize
        *not until

you accept the gift of hospitality from a lesbian
w/ mother teresa hands, break hot bread of god willing,

can you kiss up on audre lorde's poetics
                              *not until

the buzz of corner thugs who share airwaves, drunk on
dialectics — all born again from the funky duende

of concrete street life slapping against university
canon
    is when

you, poet, hone the jesus of yourself,
                          fight for
      the only name you own

called the beatdown-to-quench-the-dry throat of
reputation — letting
                your every line
                              own its mule —
your swagger salivating your brain stem — thirsting.

Saturday, a rabbit secretes outside the window of IPFW's campus, fatter, much bigger than my rabbit. I wonder if it knows the rabbit in my yard on Paulding Road? Maybe they argue about the college students, how the school continues to add building after building: the science building, the engineering building, the plans for a bridge. And maybe they don't know one another, like the rabbit outside my office window doesn't know her parents left her, had to relocate when construction took over the wooded areas that are now flat and paved and walked on by flip-flopping students looking for the future in the index and eyes of rites-of-passage, or doorways swinging in and out of the horror, obligation, how one must go on beyond the sweet clover and breasts of an overbearing mother — to press on into tomorrow. The pop-eyed rabbit — tagged Lily — shakes at field mouse, begins nibbling and preening, a WTF as to why 2-legged mammals have it so easy, don't want to accept their trails, when she has to survey a new approach out each day for nature's strict rebuff.

Working class insteps

You will glaze off inside Muzak's airy Noels,
    hold to warmth of family, as snow hairsprays over

last green of earth. Here, your ghost leaves your
    mouth, has lost the etymology to the verb "love."

On bus corner, December kicks at your head, thunder-
    storming, "keep on skully," else get slapped by barometric

stress. You wonder what bus driver philosophizes
    this chill today: Mitch, Stanley, Carlos, Vera, old Sue —

young, teeth, no teeth. The sun has walked away from you.
On bus, out window, you see a cop in Ivy Tech parking

putting antifreeze into his marked squad.
    The backpacked people & rollie-people move

to find their place inside of places. Students
    lunch-bagging futures of families to feed, & funerals

to prepare for. You feel Big Brother watches,
    you feel heat from luminations, you notice the lens,

& hear the directions from a director, but there's just space,
    just housing. Just some thrash music from the cornucopia

of student iGadgets. *They'll be stone-cold deaf in three
    years*, you think, & shift as your underwear grabs.

You carry hope like lint. There's no care. The bus driver
    hocks up a lougie — spits a sparrow from his mouth,

into the chill, while turning a corner like some Detroit
    prettyboy. *He never hits the curb.* You pull the cord

to stop burn's progression, but you are at the same
    humble you're always ending up — some beginning.

The doors open. The chill smacks cold. The corruption
    of madness dangles deep in your throat. You swallow

backwash. Spit-back "thanks brotha" to driver. Jump off.
    Git into the it.

Crossing Over the Road Not Taken
— *For Samuel Clemens and Robert Frost*

This is not the give-&-go that bounced out of bounds, that got
   tipped to the defense. This is my coach fighting for

another possession, to hold the fist & kick words I die for to
   obstruct a page, to motion eyes left to right, to jostle

craniums w/out PC juice. I don't want the fuss of my red acrylic
   canvas smears to dry up. I don't want a future voice

to smother the working voice of the past due to obfuscating
   a word that bites because it was born a bastard to

the world. I am not afraid of a word clamping its fangs into my
   muscle; I have a serum; I have a moment in my bones

that I can watch over & over on 35mm-recall, or in Blu-Ray
   HD, & I am w/ Tom Sawyer in that dark cave getting

Becky to safety, or w/ Huck, the only white person who "talks"
   to Jim like a man, but really, all I am is a middle-school

class, w/ a white woman lusciously teaching her public school
   students the sweet & sour in Twain. To read something

real, to connect w/ a life before my life was a life, & see it
   spill out, roll across page like a wave splashing back from

the Mississippi, remains the best movies I learned to access.
   Reading-rug-rats, high on southern-rug-rats living in

their true diction of those old roads — how Twain placed their
   noons & midnights before our faces, let the water slap

the rickety raft in our ears. Why crack open our skulls "now"
   to remove mortar, to unplug a Southern score?

"american us"

in that box on (5933 bunt), little nook in
wall of society, a hideaway that does not hide,
a space where ants parade on my bathroom floor
dying hundreds of deaths to a foe named d-con,
where rust sits in my dingy sink, corroding interior;
above, rain drips slowly on my thoughts, i shave
millions of tough-facial-haired people — they fall
on a color of bourbon and carbon and wash away;
when i lie on l i v i n g room floor, f a l l i n g …
i am beginning; i am ending; all at once, falling …
falling to sleep to credits that open; w a k i n g
up to credits that end; creditors end tranquility;

5933 bunt drive gets letters from the manager …
"sign a lease, if you stay month-to-month
you will pay more!" i get by a month, two, then
again, "sign a lease!" which sounds cantonese;
as much as i love the nook, i would evict the land-
lord; she encroaches, peeps in cracks; i can't be

a part of the constitution, can't be left to be; i
don't get a chance to fantasize 'bout knocks on
the door (to smile at a visitor) to welcome back
someone who i've seen in a dream on petit street —
2-doors hold me t o g e t h e r, 2-doors keep me
dissected, inside small spaces small things work;
the bible's by my bed: hughes, trethewey, brooks,
moten, and *the art of sexual healing*; my nook is
heaven, december thru march — ugly, small — me;
we embrace the cold with the thermostat at 80; the
wind whistles, runs thru wide cracks; god's arms
(my comforter)? i'm the poorest job, f a d i n g
to b l a c k , on this much-t r a v e l e d carpet.

Duen-day

"I love you in a place
Where there's no space or time"
— Donny Hathaway

He's in a heat,
eyes closed, moaning,

the smallness of piano hands
snug 'round all life's breast —

too much live ₦ die
on what he sups.

"becoming beautiful"

"To him the dismal storm appeared
The very voice of God"
—John Clare

Throwdown (reflections on fighting)
— *For Marlen Esparza*

The little girl's beast, growling behind grown woman's eyes
on laminated promos, where my scarred fists

are *boom & bam* — an alternative position —
    taped in white reinforcement, so I don't leak out.

How the fight in me is bound by
leather. Now, I control all the buttons on *this* —

relinquish all piss & pain in incremental huffs
    of combinations & fast feet.

When flat-chested, I wanted boys, so I hit them boys.
When I got breasts, I got boys, so I hit girls — my reason

    for mixing daydream-pink with pitbull-black.
In my eyes, a blood-soaked boxing ring in London Olympics.

    In my eyes, an M.D. framed in cherry wood, never dusted.
In my eyes, the blue light, feline catnip,

my want wobbling my body like a puppeteer,
the indispensable need to walk through fire, not detonate

    as blue flame wraps 'round my hard shell
because I was born with the insatiable satisfaction I am

my Papa's discontent, my Mommy's distress, my brother's
desolation, but somehow, still me. To be brawler and

    cover girl, to own the gorgeous anger of all my faces,
and to live & love all the black-eyes of the rights I cross.

"I brought you into this world …"
— *Thinkin' 'bout Reverend Marvin Pentz Gay, Sr.*

Did the strangeness of the axiom spark,
misfire after he pulled the trigger?

Was it more subtle, waiting for a police-
man to push down his head, and enter

the squad car? Did it sidle up next to him

in booking, come through collective
word play of comedians: Gregory, Cosby,

Pryor? How the stage presence of
"I'll take you out" must reverberate in

Gay, Sr.'s cranium — a preacher man
who knows God brought his boy back.

Living just enough for the city
— *"Am I my brother's keeper?"*
(Cain, Gen. 4: 9)

My mind fingers the aged pages that push
    "we could have saved lives with ifs." This

happens after loved ones die. A woulda-
    coulda-shoulda — a "if I had done this, they'd

still be animated, not ephemeral in my mind,"
    but concrete like sediment in pavement,

in loss, in the assortment of fears haunting me.
    Where I'm from, fear will cop a seat next to you

in clammy tenth-grade speech class, and project
    vociferously about breaking into a house the

night before, cooking up steaks, taking a nap,
    pilfering neighbor of mother's china and diamonds,

stuff making fear go *Wow* or *Ooo* to what's glossy.
    Fear will swivel, penetrate my eyes to caution,

grab my wrist to view the average of my Timex.
    "Cheap," fear laughs out. The bus ride home,

I grab my birthday gift, twist it round my wrist,
    think how twelfth-graders on their second go-

round never see me viable, never see waking
    the killer. Their eyes stuck on shiny brands.

January 31, 2012 (night eye)

Last night, the moon fell on me.
Yeah, the moon fell. I got all its weight.
My face against concrete, the bulging body
of the moon, flubbing against my buttocks,
copping a feel, touching old places deep
inside my keep-out-of-this-compartmental-
space-of-inhabitability. "Is the moon the
man?" I thought out rash implications,
& what I would tell my mother about being
molested by the moon. Yeah, the moon
fell on me, & all I had to give was my husk.
But the moon refused it. The molestation
was not molestation. It was frustration,
the sad in lonely. If I had no fingers or
hands or arms, how would I greet others?
How would I ask for hugs, reaching down
into the night from one big owl eye? &
how would earthlings accept me, when
we are so ugly in reflections of us?

becoming beautiful
— *For the djembe player*

but this is how it sounds in
    his head/ the reaching in the dung
for a kiss of stardust/

to bend into himself/
    let hands of ancestors thump
their aura of rise & fall

until logistics die to logic/
    goatskin/ wood body, carved calabash,
so the sweetness of cooled

fruit resonates from a Malinké
    soul/ even in Fort Wayne/ in TRIAAC loft/
he sees a Mali face on everyone's

face/ their hearts didn't stop/ the jenbe
    screams "anke djé, anke bé"/ so everyone
gathers together in peace/

in this moment of all moments, there is a
    nucleus for new moment/ here, he sees
knees, thighs, & shins are scaffolds for the body

of a West African caste/ reaching into
    murk, into tempest of light, where practice
can't hold up since in-the-moment

got her foot on practice's neck/ the slap on
    the skin recalls how color of
the past is the crayon of his now/

the moment the first two lips met/ the second
    God put papers on the drummerman,
leaving a hot sting in his fingers,

transforming the moan from jenbe body
    to the moaning of his body/ how
electricity feels, cuts him raw, a cold prison shank/

how the warmth pouring out of him gathers
    round us/ how what throbbed from him reaches
our feet, travels up, lights a dim country in our eyes

indiana saffron

driving west on
    jefferson boulevard
a buzz-cut blond-
    haired monk blurs by,
streaming in white nikes
    and his blood-orange-robe-
sorrows, leaving his
    protestant hoosier behind —
scissoring, towards
    the huge diving sun.

Amish Swag

Under his big-brimmed black hat,
he leans over a shopping cart in

Walmart, articulating a hurting
of language onto a young Amish

woman's forehead. His black suspenders
bite down on his drooping home-

made black pants. His heaven-blue
shirt, a loud plume against the dark

material. When he crosses his legs,
something James Dean-like jerks,

& rubbernecking jumps wild.
His black nike slip-ins & black socks

yell at his out-of-placeness. &, as
out of place as he tilts, he's a Don.

them teacher smoke breaks

"beyond spit-mouth boys in sagging pants.
beyond girl-karma in belly-button rings.

beyond standing in front of our students
to upset bullets. beyond dodging the

bully-shrapnel of tweens flailing their moxie.
beyond elected nouns who cut us w/ bowie-

knife-curses. the parent sighs, like fists,
for calling about their child's decline. the

fools of us, living learning like a noble verb,
before our peers do perp-walks in 6 and 10

spotlight. before *then*, turning the yellowed
pages in books on aging shelves of a librarian's

home — *that* smell. the dreamed-of places books
fed us. the way we swallowed archipelagoes

w/ orange slices, baby ruths, or bubble
yum. how we got there, we still pray that."

Blessed rancor of music
— Inspired by Cindy Cradler's #10 painting

The strings strummed in overture of Tchaikovsky
      plants dreams where a small child in me finds flight,
& fights for Decembers in a small house in Gary's

   suburb. How many houses since then have I lived
in? How many tapes & CDs have I bought to
      take me into a Russian man's mind of a ballerina's

perfect gift, one that protects her from danger?
   How those dangers get twisted up when in real life,
where we want to protect children from them, like how

      by the assimilation of the dance of the sugarplums
& the Arabian soldiers will save a child. A cold
   brings chill, makes me readjust under Mama's quilt.

I have traveled to worlds, to other children's dreams,
      in my drowsiness. I hear Nat King Cole singing
"tiny tots with their eyes all aglow," & hear that

   connection to us all, know too how a song from
one man belongs to many. Now the chubby-jawed
      jazz man, Mel Tormé, waves to me, along with

Ebenezer & Rudolph & Ralphie. They're things
   in my drowsiness — how I got here. The music
snuggles me into slumber. The tree's manipulation

      with lights. A decorative soldier, positioned
around strings of rainbow bulbs & garland, winks to me
   under blurred cacophony of family voices, as

I pursue a nap on the couch in the home my mother
        bought back in the '70s. How the home can save us
from what flurries life. How devout the beauty of voices

        that clamor with the smells of coming back.
I own the noise, that heartbeat reverberating against the body
        of the couch. That head space, & all its children.

"becoming beautiful"

Jean-Michel Basquiat's
Boyhood Song

I stepped on the cracks of sidewalks,
"not scared to break my mama's back,"

not scared to know all time and space,
not scared to do what I must do, no matter

what daddy said. Life was the same ole
same ole, so I started painting my mind

on concrete New York sidewalks. I started
reading and reading, then reading more,

as if I would die if I couldn't capture words
in a peanut butter jar. I started spilling

my guts in crayon on New York buildings
'cause I didn't have the proper backyard

to play in. I accepted paint brushes as my
fingers and people as my toys and books

as real life 'cause the fire-spark in me blew
up like I had thrown up magical colors

that angels painted on rainbows. And
the music, the music that pumps its beat,

the music that thumps in my chest
has my brave heart looking to accept the rain,

the sun, the moon, to become the-king-
of-okay. I am okay — the joy-joy star.

The closest I got to superhero

was when a spider bit me twice on
my top lip. I was in dream. I didn't
awake with tingling Spidey powers.
Radioactivity unplugged, I guess.
For all I thought about were the eggs
it laid inside me. How I was pregnant
and could spout my manly pregnancy
to all. *Is that a superpower, being
pregnant and male?* Maybe I could
go around promoting my womanist-
maleness, lactating over power tools
in the hardware aisle at Sears, while
thinking about the half-off sale in shoes,
or the new Martha Stewart prints in
Home & Garden. Maybe I would be
the gun-toting, red-lipstick Mama male
bear, hunting, wearing two gun belts
on my birthing hips over my pleated
and plaid kilt, my earth-toned blouse
with two belts of bullets crisscrossing
over my baby bump full of spider kids.
Would my babies bump inside my lip?

When a spider bit me there, twice,
it looked like a cold sore, herpes
at first, and I tried Campho-Phenique,
Blistex, the universal Vaseline. It brought
a shine to my bulbous mound. I used
medicated powder. There's nothing
like a brown man with white lips. *Talk
less*, I said like a sage. As the pronged
bite marks started throbbing, I knew
Peter Parker and I would never network,
bypassing each other, web-slinging on

white ash and pine trees of my city of
no skyscrapers. I knew my haters wouldn't
be named Electro, Doc Ock, or Rhino.
The fools disliking me, called Dollar Bill, T.C.
and Sugar Baby — love the movie, not the
book — carry extra clips because ammo
legislates streets like Congress. They'd
make fun of me, my pregnant lip. I vibrate
with no Spidey halo. I burn in my anger,
not "super" nor "hero," yet somehow, I
still swing on drab prayers of repentance,
hope they will shimmer out, gold webs.

"deep life"

"*I dream excess — high-speed vision. Snow falling upwards.*"
—Erica Hunt

9/11/2010
— R.I.P. SC, Sr.

A "holy man" in Florida cares to burn Qurans
today, tugs at ripe media flash — cheap fear in some.

    Like some burned Anne Frank, Angelou, Rowlings,
some want to even burn all bibles not King James.

A friend, Emmanuel, will poet manna of Latino matins,
    a bouncing reverb off harmonic walls in TRIAAC's loft,

nine years later on this rainy anniversary,
when skyline of NY's clean-shaven from planes' blades.

    So you, Grandpa, Mississippi boy, must sign up on
grief's waiting-list. Everyone's right & wrong all at once.

& since we only talked at funerals — your son's — the man
    who left my mama his name, a baby me. Your grandson's —

my legit half-brother & your second son's — "the good kid."
Now, who will I laugh clumsily w/ of the curse on family males

    if you're in opal casket? I shared the night w/ Emmanuel,
when a poem rustled me down. On FB, Calibri font slapped

upside my eyes, "You going to your grandfather's funeral?"
    A hit collapsing me to a sack, a landslide of earth on my chest,

my breath taken by friend on FB — someone who volunteers
the 411 — someone not knowing there's no poem to treat

    what I correctly feel, no verb big enough to paint
my metaphors of graffitied fusion. There's only what it is,

"deep life"

you & I knotted in DNA's trust. I'm heir, running after
    our skein of yarn. My life rolls to its end, as you dream less

in pin-striped double-breasted. So untouchable, the dead,
the Twin Towers, the rescue workers, the volunteers. I think …

   burning books w/ this *rain?* Takes me where books connected
us. Dr. Seuss's magical words via mama's mailbox. Now

my words got talons — grown alphabet from book spines & dead.

deep life

i.
The marine biologist before us, a modern Moses parting
a Red Sea, said *the same dolphin that you think is smiling
at you has the same smile when it kills you.* Referring
to why animal lovers believe *tursiops truncatus* are cute,
harmless. *We never hear from the ones that get killed,* he
said, face down. I stood on a ridge, ocean up to my waist,
with "the ones that get killed" hurtling their magic of
Poseidon's water sorcery against my brown body, catching
and dropping instructions on how not to upset the 400-
pound swimming life-form from the movie *Zeus and
Roxanne,* when a trainer's sleek hand gesture made the
dolphin sluice himself into Atlantic, then blast up out of
the ocean to sheen in a slo mo, sun kissing a silver bullet —
slipping through God's hands, shot out like a shot, back
down into cerulean depths — somewhere African skeletons
lay mannequin, bodymeat eaten by bottom feeders. The
bottlenose, clever escape artist from clever tiger sharks
who crave silver rump, just another survivor in salt water
named by gods. The dolphin pirouettes on watery stage.
Long spray of ocean's starburst tears spun in a watery
maypole, dropped back wet into itself. In the Atlantic,
beauty lives in small matter — bottom feeders atop human
skeletons. It's all life. It's all death. To live like my
bottlenose brother, I must die for Atlantic's beautiful drink.

ii.
I look at the ocean differently now that I've had a relation-
ship with its blue eyes and tossing hips. Riding a trail horse
from Freeport into Atlantic's mouth solidified my excite-
ment. I was struck by the dark horse's mane and neck
entering the turquoise of wet nerve endings, bringing back
black forearmed boatman whose veins keloid out like a
whipped slave's back — possible progeny of similar black

hands that feed Santo Domingo with bodies, and relocated. He took a gaggle of us Americans to where dolphins recoup in the aquamarine — waters where myth moves beyond all comprehension. Fuss about our makeup decomposes in the ocean's bed, where fool, fisherman, drug runner, and slave sleep without worry of conception, all our eyes awe-reflecting.

Oscar sits on his lawn chair like a monarch butterfly,
cross-legged, puffing on non-filters. If he had wings

they'd be folding over him like a quilt — he'd be non-
compliant in orange. He concludes this life near whom-

ever's perching next to him. He learned the faces of
Paulding Road — will not invade the tiny space in names.

We all need some distance. He will acknowledge
new management of Twin Oaks Apartments; he speaks

with iffy immigrants cleaning up paper and cans and
thrown shrapnel around odiferous garbage bins; he

consorts with Five-O, who sets speed traps, branding
hot tickets at lunchtime; he chats under fumes with fire-

men who siren their way through the pallid smoke in
his apartment complex; he knows that the green Lexus

sitting on 22s belongs to *recalcitrant butthole* living
off burn-out mom in apartment 2B, who gives her son

all her pocket change, living in her big guilt. Oscar is
more mudbone; youngster's more hardhead. None

of this upsets the man whose spine twists in puzzles,
veins fight off sugar, and a toothlessness so pronounced

dark gums give him integrity. Frisco the squirrel, and
how Frisco lost her mate, bent Oscar over. Oscar saw

the cobalt car smack her mate out, then a car of flame, then
a car of clouds. He lost colors in speed of a colorwheel.

When he sees Frisco, he waves her over, and they choke
on how God's so close — untouchable.

"deep life"

Sound

Simple as this wheat spooling
into itself; a dangling hair-glop
in my husband's senior picture.
This bold silence walks through wheat
looking for rest, while three men strip
my hardwood oak floors like grafts
on burn victims. But all burns aren't
made by fire. Men say they will save
the wood, but can the oak tree be saved
by *this* time? Silence stomps. Silence
waits on this plane, ready to take away
the wind pushing its back. There's no
shrieking. My husband cannot see
this bully; he is lock-jawed to what
our parents have planted; to what
settlers called *prime dirt* and *home*,
and he wishes change would change
its mind, but what does a man know
about this wind, a woman, amnesty?
It's as simple as the curling wheat
spooning itself into little laughters
and cooing to the west. The three
men and my husband conspire to rule
the land, thinking, *wheat does not
become wheat without me.* They do
not know they conspire. Men only see
above the earth; never the life of
her seed. What's left, a man's shame
of gutting her and her children —
reminder holes pumped full of *okays*
and *I understands*. But do men ever
strip their own skin, feel one-hundred-
year nails subtracted from their
bodies? Or do they sand bumpy

notches and buff and buff and
buff 'til the wind defends herself
for letting the wheat say, "ahh?"

Velvet shock therapy

Loud as he roared, he could wear silence
like a gunslinger — a quiet acquaintance —
delicate as the velvet red pillow a lover gave
him before he would depart into his mind.
Born in Georgia's good genes, a neo-southern
gentleman, he often twitched his red-haired
eyelids when reciting in its entirety the *Song
of Myself,* or gave insight (to the party-goers)
how Ginsberg whispered in Cassidy's dream,
in some sullied bar on the outskirts of El Paso
Kerouac loved each woman he planted with his
gift. He questioned Zondervan's reconstruction
of God's Beatitudes, and even how Job crumbled.
He was full of electricity from voltage-therapy
to stop him from kissing other men. Those glitches
in his brilliance — eye spasms — brain synapses
are the small connections to the Renaissance, Rome,
and religion. How wild should the torture from
your own family be? To make things resonate
true like a lily's lip, does it take heartache
in a suffering? He suffered each wave of river's
rippling thrum, burning his strange words to
moonglow in my memory box, a vexing voice,
a language lost to burnt shadow casting itself
onto itself, a night swallowed in blackness,
leaving the man in his boyhood composite,
eyelids like popping flashbulbs.

Identity Thief
— *For Deborah K. Littlejohn*

What's this strange word that's moved in
with you? I told you, "stay clear of strange

nouns who only have death in their marrow."
He's horrid, makes you puny, fusses ardently

with your immune system, has it betray, usurp
your tries at forgiveness. He wants you splotchy

like a bruised ripe juicy peach or an Asian pear.
The first time you said his name, I thought you

said, "Lucus." A name more fitting of a noun —
a noun who could easily relax his breath on nape

of your neck. But "Lupus" is pallid, a buff, a taker.
I know it, you know it, each physician knows it.

What can we do? He loves you and you don't give
in, unless he's hung over in bed, then you're drawn

to warm sunlight in your big bay window. John,
your neighbor, tells me how musically your body

meets mature warmth — your nakedness is shaky
but your elusive smile shows how your limbs arc

and speak truth, are honest in sunlight. One by
one, more neighbors peep in on you — they don't

subside, they wish you'd open your front door, run
into each of their arms. Your smile gets confused.

John. The neighbors. They scatter. Wonder
"why does she play *that* game?" John calls. Tells

me about sun rolling into blue; how neighbors
had you again until cocky Lupus raised his hand.

Black Whiskers

She points to the filmed big one atop
of its brothers. Another customer
points through the display window asking,
"How much for the whiting in back?"
Sunday's noon sun glimmers sleek
luminous blackness on white paper.
There is a string uncut that connects
head to body. Severed guts drip
to ooze richness. A smell rises
to raise a pungent slap. "I need six
of them for soup," a woman yells.
He looks out a window not missing
his mark, aware of life. Residue of
the counter sparkling with catfish heads.
She turns away, far away, to Great Lakes
and green intentions of their marble eyes.
Her keen son touches a black whisker
smearing a smudge on the glass display
window with film of death. Red licorice
moist from heat in the boy's mouth growls
a stomach to hunger. Supper is six in
the evenings when day has deheated.
The man leaves his knife settled in cutting
board, paper wraps heads together,
links gray matter, and wipes his hands
on soiled red apron.

block party

clean & grimy tasting
baptist-heads next door
packing heat & tatts
some witnesses
pseudoephedrine & meth
muslim & hurt
zionist & mormon
dreamsicle some
next door to me
"white" & "black"
very few swallow trust
few italian few irish
drive bro's old regal
some drive caddies
drive suv's next door
some shrimp-fried rice
drive debt to its peak
some have migraines
some high in depression
some take valium
jewish & urban
next door to me?

next door to me
tv sad starlookers
dependently independent
get dementia
buddhist-born
some take zoloft
junkmailin' & b ballin'
tv tired thieves
happy cheaters
fussy gyro kings
a few get electrotherapy
chuck taylors on concrete
insides crisp from chemo
some drive camrys
one or two know good tv
drive farmers hard
some work other's nerves
membrane's gone
suburban & baha'i
got alzheimer's
forgot to forget
america's america

republican & liars
some bus exhaust
flip flops & pizza eaters
some drive prii
native american & ho
devout & gay
sinners & democrats
few swallow trust
i-don't-give-a-damners
"hispanic" & "brown"
lipstick soccer moms
cubano or mexicano
burmese & indian
devout & searching
drive dad's f-150
drive bills to the roof
some take percocet
catholic next door
african & german
a race[ing] nation
move like lizards
next door to me

"deep life"

A train is gon' come (elegy for the big afro)
— *R.I.P. Don Cornelius*

Did music's blood-soul stop coagulating?
Were you still pissed at Motown's mess?

    Still pissed at Philadelphia breaking its fever?
    Or, did a woman push your heart outside?

        O'Bryan's rustlin' falsettos & so much
        thumpin' erupts today as the afro of the deep-

voiced brotha stands as tall as Jermaine
& four other Jacksons — mountains of hair

fighting for a protagonist part in this new lens.
All that hair bounced w/ back beats, spins,

    splits — the pageantry of loud clothes smiling.
    All that hair like mine — nappy, teased &

        greased to please when coming up off
        the floor, to go back down, to git up, again.

    Soul ran thru the mic, arcing into your mouth,
    buzzing thru your veins. *How do you*

master the masters, Don? How do you hold
black, put "diamond in the back, sunroof

    top, diggin' the scene with a gangsta lean"
    when JB's hot-sweating-off slave-puddles

        on your stacks & bells? Do you wash away
        that drench, or do you fold those pants up,

    keep them like interest on 401Ks? I have
not felt the gravel — no rocks in throat like

"This" Ameri-can-*ah*

this since Grandma Marie moved into earth,
or Cochese died, & Preach finds him under

    Chi-town's train viaducts. Everything on
    Cooley High soundtrack is "a stone-cold blast,"

        is black-life dancing on master's grave —
        is a broken strut stolen from shoutin' days,

    where tail feathers, shaking, are hold-up
    guns, where Godfather of Soul said we

have to beat the beat tender if we want
to catch that beat on the one — beginnings.

    So I am blowing off thick dust bunnies,
pulling out albums, reading water-damaged

liner notes, again —
        romancing
            that smell in home —
    blue-gray sutures pokin' heart.

The third child

Your mother, puffed to pathetic
eyes, looked down on you
like God laughs on us all —
disappointment lingering
like cumulus clouds, pallid
and thick. Your limp left arm
bothers her mind, and prayers
aren't paying off enough to
move brachial nerve damage
to where mothers never wear worry.
In white bassinet, prayers circle,
a strange mobile above your sleep —
so thick, your mother sees
notes in the dawn releasing from
her mouth up to God. She wants you
to have delicious days,
promising nights. Now, it's done.

Now, it's gone, and you've become
heavy phrasing: "little missy,"
"bad as hell," "my sweetie pie."
Then, because of worry, she felt
she shoved you into this world,
out of her, too soon, too fast.
Now, the arm that flopped
about catches you from falling to
the then you never knew, and
has your mother yelling, "you got
yo hands in everything!" You leave
dejected, but later, healed by a mother's
forehead kiss, you sleep. Your
mother smiles, knows you run well
with trouble. But now, she's tight
with Heaven, rubs the tired out of her

eyes, and the residue of wetness
is a lotion she rubs into her hands.

Awake

We barefoot on this red plot,
sow and knead her hips and thighs,
tender with her old loins. See, she
our young days, we her blue skies.

Gangsta love
— *For all the Jean-Michel Basquiats*

I wouldn't want to know you on drug days
when you were in a stupor of dumb thought
& I had to clean you up — take off the pissy
pants & underwear, the vomited-on T-shirt
your moms gave you that's too little, but is love,
the discord of language you spat out like a
Tourette-induced aggravation. I wouldn't want
to know you on the mad days where you throw
paint against old canvases & let the music of
Vivaldi or Grandmaster Flash push you into
locomotion, because critics critiqued you all
wrong. I wouldn't want to know the man who
couldn't put the love on his woman, & was
always kicked to the curb with her abusive
foot-to-the-groin reverberations of let-downs.

& on any given moon, I would sit by the bed
while you slept off the voices, look into world
of your paint splatters, love you back to raw.

Midwest hang, man

We park like trumpeter swans in Monticello, Minnesota,
maybe because it's a meeting spot for singles, or maybe

because we're still cygnets, our minds drawn to things
shiny. We will park to park — it's our duty, to have

a break away from our arduous gold lives. We park
on the strip, at multi-plex in a strip mall, the Dairy Queen,

at beaches, by high school bleachers, in Walgreen's parking
lot, under marquee gas station burnt out by midnight,

at the Steak 'n Shake, the Denny's (open 24/7). We park.
We park in our odd postures, as we hate and love good

and bad (cats and dogs for life) — we park. We park
to show off our father's mint '57 T-Bird, older brother's

ardor for Chevelle, hot crotch-rockets, mopeds, hoopties,
or used Mustangs we bought as our first find, using dinero

we made in the high school havoc of sound investing with
homework, broken dates, b-ball games. We know all cops,

their blue intentions (dream blue with their kids) in a city's
grand design to speed trap us, trip us up. In avoidance,

we are loudest. We park in the muggy heat, stinging rain-
storms, the snow, nippy autumn. We park so grown-ups'll

get jealous when they see us, cry out *disrespectful, stupid*
when they get caught in the loop, recalling days they got

felt up, or felt down — to see what they've created from
firm foundations. It is not smoke, Bud, Coca-Cola

(that runs through us), we need stability; we pray, park
on dirt roads, on concrete our predecessors paved,

imprinting with new weight the footprints belonging
to dangling bronze shoes hanging from a rearview.

A Pen Pal with HIV Gets Lost in Shuffle

I pitched your letters for kindling. I had concealed them in a plastic Kmart
bag inside my closet, next to the brothers & sisters of letters from people

who mailed their voices to me through the U.S. Postal Service. I hadn't seen
your face until this poem stood up to yawn, stretching its taut body, taking

me back before emails, & texting. An X-girl-friend with anger in her throat,
a fine Hoosier, planted ear bombs, & made me toss all my letters from females,

or in fancy penmanship. She found a plastic bag on an inventory sweep to
my "true identity," which sounds better in her fiction for me. Even if I hadn't

slept with the female authors, felt their unclothed pelvises & strong legs,
open, around my unclothed hips; even when letters were of an agape nature,

my X, misrepresenting God, full to the tilt with male friends from work &
college, full in her totem pole of Xs herself, questioned all the words from

sisters, aunts, Mom, friends — like you. There is regret to grapple with here,
for I was burnt by an arsonist, a denial & a "why the hell did I do that?" But

I still picture pictures where your smiles leave my throat a lump — how
HIV couldn't strap you down. You let me in on your new boy toy, as

pleased as I was, as marred as I was. For it would be arduous in all little
things. Spontaneity would be planned like beach folk do for hurricanes.

Or, there'd be the talk of all talks to let him know how if he wanted to play
on your bandstand, he would need to read an instruction manual on your hazel

irises. Somehow I remember those, how strong they veered off the pics. Or,
how you'd say "If anything, I'm up front now. So dangerous ... I have to be."

If you were me, you'd have all your letters — all the words lived & sent out —
no trinkets, but lifelines sleeping in a tired blue box next to pressed butterflies.

Six dandelions beg for some sun, off the I-65

i. uncle
There's a man in your forehead
tugging at the pulley attached to your eyebrow;

he's on the second floor above
the eye, foot pushing down on awning-eyelid —

something turns to mean.

There's a man inside your hand,
swatting at flies, but the flies are people, and he can't

    notice a difference.

There's a man inside your "acidy" stomach,
running uphill, a slippery hamster, stung, screaming,

making your stomach growl,

    but the body on the outside sizzles.

ii. daughter
        There's a girl sluggin' it out with some-
        one who is her spittin' image. It looks

        like the windmill technique, two flailing

        arms spinning, praying for some contact —

        when she connects, there's two hers

        on the ground: one broken,
        the other, slivers of mirror.

iii. aunt
You have waited eight birthdays for
some peace. From your third tall boy,

a belch dives out your mouth, some
acidic reflux, then you smile. This may

be the closest you have gotten to euphoria,
smelling it in hops and barley and pizza.

Your son's in the smoke from your cig,
only a ghost, where you blow out stress.

iv. son

        There's a boy wrestling a man
        thinking it's an angel, thinking

        he's a man, thinking how thinking's
        got him into this big fight of all time.

        He throws some haymakers, connecting
        each time to the man who's like an angel.

        He ducks. The angel-man misses.
        Then he throws two left jabs, a left cross

        to confuse the angel's right side, and
        when the angel-dude adjusts, it gets

        a right to the chin, knocking the power
        out of its legs. Sprawled out all over

        the ground like slow water from a hose,
        he looks up to a twin, an angry boy

taunting down at him. The boy raises
hateful fists — no good to come his way.

v. mother
There is a woman whose past reaches to pull
her back, but she's a grown gazelle, and knows

how cheetahs can never go the distance. Although
tired, this is flight or fight, she's avoiding those

semi-retractable claws wanting to grip antelope
meat — those days when she was lost in a stasis

of depression — it all wants her down, to grow
the derooted talons back into the cilia of every

smallness she owns. Her daughter cannot see
this, due to the camouflage on mom's skin; she

thinks "mom is just mean," "noncommittal," "old."
Mom thinks young gazelles take too many chances,

relying on foolishness and speed, while even
she and mature ilk run in the same circles,

> never able to catch a breath, 'less it be the last.

vi. father
> I am mad. I have put myself into
> this wheel, hamstering around a life

> I can never control. Others live here,
> too. We bump and bump against glass.

"deep life"

Would rather be out there with those
big brown eyes, magnifying how sideshow

it all is. I could scratch out those eyes,
even in my littleness, on the outside.

So I wait. Work the wheel. Get shoulders
strong. When eyes not on me, I spin wheel,

and sharpen my claws, just waiting until
eyes clean my cage. Then, I will pounce.

Magic Man

Some say my skin has this power to   magnetize
bullets   towards my blue veins, but   I have never

been a stickup kid, or Houdini. They say my skin
has this strength that scares guns into the hands of

those who see "danger" — a brown face in hoodie,
even if it's cold out & I'd rather warm my ears

from these mad winds. My skin makes some white
men lock up daughters & wives, in this "post-racial"

apocalypse. I never knew   this pigment could scream
at women to clutch purses as if babies — horrified, even

when my lips don't move. I never knew this epidermis
could make the word "nigger" swell up to ogre size,

have some policemen shrink to ants   in the shadow
of my huge carbon footprint.   when all I ever did,

slide out   my mama's womb,   brown, in an
amniotic fluid, yell — 'cause the doctor put his hands

on me. As ooo-&-ah-cute as I was to "all," a spring
popped loose in the interim, & the "all" harshly rubbed

their red eyes. A taint wasted — a backwash — a sour
after-taste in humanity, like drinking orange juice

after the systematic brushing of teeth. There's no way
to sugarcoat the bitterness in this life's lemonade. Today,

life's prepped me on who can touch this brownness.
The man. The mirror. Me. I still see   my cute boy.

This   gift,   my Mama   gave y'all.

ABOUT THE AUTHOR

Curtis L. Crisler was born and raised in Gary, Indiana. He received a BA in English, with a minor in theater, from Indiana University-Purdue University Fort Wayne (IPFW), and he received an MFA from Southern Illinois University Carbondale. His poetry chapbook, *Black Achilles*, will be released in 2015 by Accents Publishing. His previous books are: *Pulling Scabs* (nominated for a Pushcart), *Tough Boy Sonatas* (young adult), and *Dreamist: a mixed-genre novel* (young adult). His chapbooks are *Wonderkind* (nominated for a Pushcart), *Soundtrack to Latchkey Boy*, and *Spill* (which won the 2008 Keyhole Chapbook Award). He is the recipient of a residency at the City of Asylum/Pittsburgh (COA/P), the recipient of fellowships from Cave Canem, Virginia Center for the Creative Arts, and Soul Mountain, and he was a guest resident at Hamline University. He edited the nonfiction book, *Leaving Me Behind: Writing a New Me*, on the Summer Bridge experience at IPFW. Crisler received the Sterling Plumpp First Voices Poetry Award, two Indiana Arts Commission Grants, and the Eric Hoffer Award, and was nominated for the Eliot Rosewater Award. His poetry has been adapted for theatrical productions in New York and Chicago, and he has been published in a variety of magazines, journals, and anthologies. Crisler is an associate professor of English at IPFW.